The Biggest Pet

by Carmel Reilly

illustrated by Jack Viant
and Daniel Hawkins

OXFORD
UNIVERSITY PRESS
AUSTRALIA & NEW ZEALAND

It was pet day at school.
Everybody was very excited.

Evelyn peered into the classroom.
Her friend, Darcy, had his dog, Duke.
Grace had her goldfish, Gem.

Charlotte had her cat, Chef.

Harry had Harvey the hairy hamster.

However, no one had a **BIG** pet...
except Evelyn. Her pet was called Eddie.

Eddie was **VERY** big.
In fact, Eddie was **HUGE**!
Eddie was a **MASSIVE** grey...

ELEPHANT!

"My goodness!" said Mrs Chute as Eddie stomped by. "What an impressive pet you have. He's so...big!"

"He is," agreed Evelyn. "He is so big that he has to live outside in our garden!"

Just then Eddie the elephant crashed into a desk.

Harvey, the hairy hamster, went flying.

Harvey landed on Duke, the dog. Duke let out a loud bark.

Chef, the cat, got a fright. She leapt out the window.

It was chaos!

Mrs Chute and the children raced outside.
Eddie stomped out behind them.

They looked around for Chef.

Chef!

Evelyn stopped by the bicycle shed and looked up.

"Look!" said Evelyn. "Chef is on the bicycle shed roof!"

"We have to get her down," cried Charlotte.

"I will get a ladder from the gym," said Mrs Chute.

"No need, Mrs Chute," said Evelyn.
"Eddie and I can get Chef."

"Eddie, will you give me a lift?" asked Evelyn.

When Eddie put his trunk out, Evelyn stepped lightly on it.

Eddie lifted Evelyn into the air. Now she could easily reach the roof.

Chef was crouched low.

"Do not fear," called Evelyn. "We will get you down."

Evelyn gently picked Chef up. Eddie lowered them down.

Evelyn gave the cat back to her friend.
Everybody cheered.

Evelyn lifted Eddie's ear. "You are the biggest pet," she whispered, "and we are very best friends!"